LANGUAGE !® is a trademark of Jane Fell Greene, Ed.D.
Degrees of Reading Power®, DRP®, and DRP→BookLink® are registered trademarks of Touchstone Applied Science Associates, Inc.

Text layout and design by Kim Harris
Cover design by Becky Malone
Production Assistance by Denise Geddis

ISBN 1-57035-233-X

Printed in the United States of America

Published and Distributed by

SOPRIS
WEST
EDUCATIONAL SERVICES

4093 Specialty Place • Longmont, CO 80504 • (303) 651-2829
www.sopriswest.com

120BKC

Contents

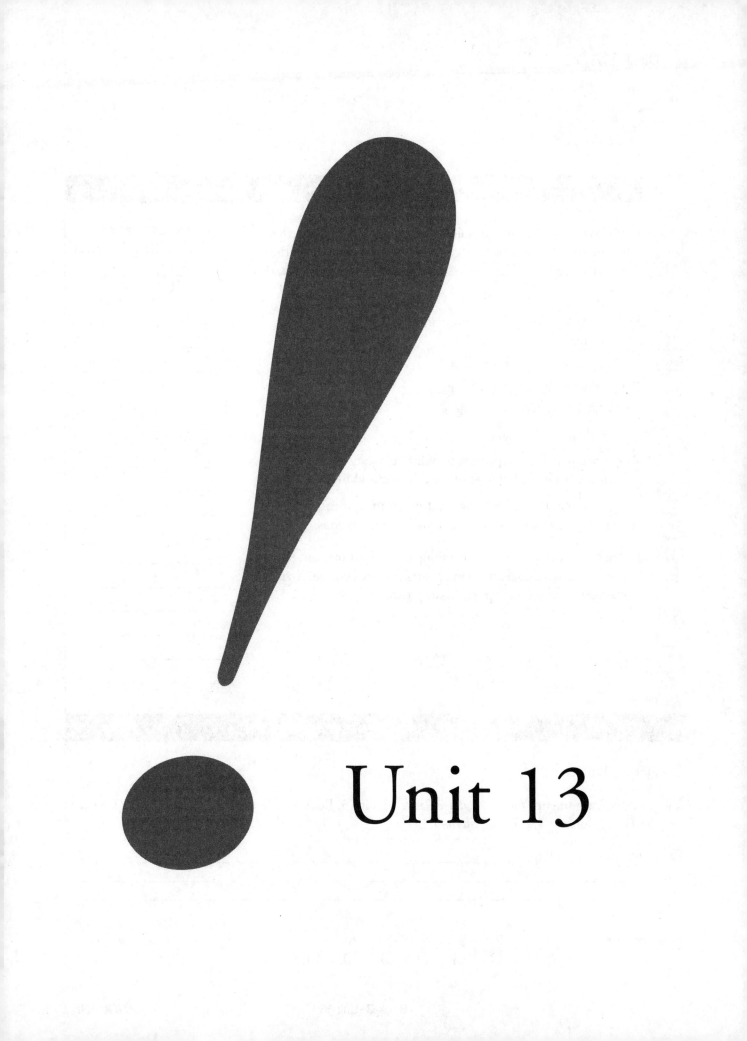

Unit 13

Map

CONCEPTS & CONTENT	NOTES & EXAMPLES

READING

SPELLING

❑ **Blends** are consonant combinations that are welded together before or after the vowel in a syllable. Each consonant in the blend is sounded. The inside sound is the one that is hardest to "hear."

❑ Phoneme-grapheme correspondences in this unit: Consonant combinations

- **l** blends: **bl**, **gl**, **cl**, **pl**, **fl**, **sl**
- **r** blends: **br**, **fr**, **tr**, **cr**, **dr**, **gr**, **pr**, **shr**, **thr**
- **s** blends: **sc**, **sm**, **sn**, **sp**, **sk**, **st**
- **w** blends: **sw**, **tw**, **dw**

Letter pairs that represent two different consonant phonemes at the beginning of a word are called **initial blends**.

Consonant combinations are difficult to segment. Both consonant sounds are heard in initial blends.

❑ **Analysis** questions require breaking down information. Some specific words signal an Analysis question: **categorize**, **sort**, **classify**, **arrange**, **compare**, **distinguish**.

ACTIVITIES, ASSIGNMENTS & ASSESSMENT

❑ Fluency Builders   1   2   3   4

❑ Reading Assignment: *J & J Language Readers* Unit 13, Book 1: *The Class Trip*; Book 2: *A Thrill at the Track*; Book 3: *The Twins' Swim Trip*

❑ Independent Reading: _____

_____

_____

Mastery Tasks   1   2   3   4   5   6   7
                     ❑   ❑   ❑   ❑   ❑   ❑   ❑

CONCEPTS & CONTENT	NOTES & EXAMPLES

❑ Six Traits of Effective Writing:
Focus:

- Word Choice

- Sentence Fluency

    A description is designed to evoke an image in the mind of the reader.

❑ **Adjectives** are words that describe nouns. Adjectives tell which, what kind of, or how many.
Examples:

- **Which**: a, the, this, that

- **What kind of**: long, hot, slim, flat

- **How many**: six, ten, less

❑ Noun possessive:

- Adding ' + <u>s</u> shows ownership (possession) of the noun.

- Singular: <u>-'s</u> (**cat, cat's**); Plural: <u>-s'</u> (**cats, cats'**)

❑ Masterpiece Sentence
Focus: Stage 4: Paint Your Subject
This stage develops the understanding and use of adjectives.
The subject of a sentence can be expanded by asking **what kind**, **which**, or **how many**.

WRITING & ENGLISH LANGUAGE ARTS

ACTIVITIES, ASSIGNMENTS & ASSESSMENT

❑ Composition Assignment: _____

_____

_____

Mastery Tasks   8   9   10   11   12   13
                      ❑   ❑   ❑   ❑   ❑   ❑

Instructional Content

WORDS TO READ/SPELL

l blends	r blends	s blends	w blends	Other	Nonphonetic Words
black	Brad	skill	twin	thong	*they*
blocks	brag	smash	swim		*your*
clam	brick	smell			
clap	brim	snack			
class	brisk	snap			
clock	crab	sniff			
flag	crash	spill			
flap	cross	spot			
flat	drag	stack			
flock	drinks	stand			
glad	drop	stick			
glib	fresh	sticks			
flash	grill	stiff			
plan	prick	still			
plot	shrank	stink			
slack	shrill				
slash	thrill				
slim	trick				
	trip				
	trash				

EXPANDED WORD LIST

blab	clef	flab	gloss	prop	slit	stab
bled	click	fled	grab	scab	slob	staff
blip	cliff	flesh	grab bag	scads	slog	stag
bliss	cling	flex	grass	scam	slosh	stash
blob	clink	flick	grid	scan	slot	stem
block	clip	fling	grim	scoff	smack	step
blot	clod	flip	grin	scuff	smock	sting
blush	clog	flip-flop	grip	shred	smog	stock
brad	clop	flit	grit	shrink	smut	stop
bran	clot	flog	grits	slab	snag	twig
brash	cloth	flop	grog	slack	snip	
brass	crack	floss	o'clock	slag	snob	
brat	cram	Fred	plank	slam	span	
bred	crib	fret	pled	slang	spank	
brig	criss-cross	frill	plod	slap	spat	
bring	crock	frizz	plop	slat	sped	
broth	crop	frock	prank	sled	spell	
clack	drab	frog	prep	slick	spin	
clad	dress	from	press	slid	spin off	
clan	drip	glad rags	prim	sling	spit	
clang	drum	glass	prom	slink	spit up	
clash	dwell	glob	prong	slip	spot-check	

FIVE FAVORITE IDIOMS OR EXPRESSIONS

1. _____

2. _____

3. _____

4. _____

5. _____

Tasks for Mastery

READING

Student Mastery Score	Minimum Mastery Score	Maximum Mastery Score
	24	**30**
80% or more correct, progress to next Task.		

TASK 1: **Phoneme Segmentation**

Listen to the words your teacher says. In the following blanks, write 3, 4, 5, or 6 to tell how many different phonemes (sounds) you hear in each word.

1. _____ 2. _____ 3. _____ 4. _____ 5. _____ 6. _____

7. _____ 8. _____ 9. _____ 10. _____ 11. _____ 12. _____

13. _____ 14. _____ 15. _____ 16. _____ 17. _____ 18. _____

19. _____ 20. _____ 21. _____ 22. _____ 23. _____ 24. _____

25. _____ 26. _____ 27. _____ 28. _____ 29. _____ 30. _____

Unit 13 Tasks for Mastery (continued)

Student Mastery Score	Minimum Mastery Score	Maximum Mastery Score
	24	30
80% or more correct, progress to next Task.		

TASK 2: **Listening for Blends**

Listen to the words your teacher says. In the following blanks, write the initial blend you hear. As you write each blend, pronounce its sounds aloud.

1. _____ 2. _____ 3. _____ 4. _____ 5. _____ 6. _____

7. _____ 8. _____ 9. _____ 10. _____ 11. _____ 12. _____

13. _____ 14. _____ 15. _____ 16. _____ 17. _____ 18. _____

19. _____ 20. _____ 21. _____ 22. _____ 23. _____ 24. _____

25. _____ 26. _____ 27. _____ 28. _____ 29. _____ 30. _____

Student Mastery Score	Minimum Mastery Score	Maximum Mastery Score
	20	25
80% or more correct, progress to next Task.		

TASK 3: **Listening for Word Parts**

Listen to each word. Write the word part that your teacher repeats to you.

1. _____ 2. _____ 3. _____ 4. _____ 5. _____

6. _____ 7. _____ 8. _____ 9. _____ 10. _____

11. _____ 12. _____ 13. _____ 14. _____ 15. _____

16. _____ 17. _____ 18. _____ 19. _____ 20. _____

21. _____ 22. _____ 23. _____ 24. _____ 25. _____

Student Mastery Score	Minimum Mastery Score	Maximum Mastery Score
	2	2
80% or more correct, progress to next Task.		

TASK 4: **Nonphonetic Words**

The Unit 13 nonphonetic words are **they** and **your**. How would each word sound if it were phonetically regular?

they _____   your _____

SPELLING

Student Mastery Score	Minimum Mastery Score	Maximum Mastery Score
	19	24
80% or more correct, progress to next Task.		

TASK 5: **Letter Pairs**

The Unit 13 words have initial consonant blends. Write some of the words in the following categories.

dr-   **cr-**   **st-**   **tr-**   **bl-**   **sm-**

_____   _____   _____   _____   _____   _____

_____   _____   _____   _____   _____   _____

br-   **gl-**   **fl-**   **sn-**   **sp-**   **cl-**

_____   _____   _____   _____   _____   _____

_____   _____   _____   _____   _____   _____

Student Mastery Score	Minimum Mastery Score	Maximum Mastery Score
	17	21
80% or more correct, progress to next Task.		

TASK 6: **Spelling Word List**

Write the words that your teacher dictates on the Spelling Practice forms in the back of this book.

Student Mastery Score	Minimum Mastery Score	Maximum Mastery Score
	4	5
80% or more correct, progress to next Task.		

TASK 7: **Spelling Mastery Sentences**

1. _____

   _____

2. _____

   _____

3. _____

   _____

4. _____

   _____

5. _____

   _____

ENGLISH/LANGUAGE ARTS

Student Mastery Score	Minimum Mastery Score	Maximum Mastery Score
	10	12
80% or more correct, progress to next Task.		

TASK 8: **Nouns and Verbs**

Some words can be nouns or verbs. In the following blanks, use each word:
(1) as a noun, and (2) as a verb.

plot

1. (N) _____

2. (V) _____

stand

3. (N) _____

4. (V) _____

flash

5. (N) _____

6. (V) _____

lock

7. (N) _____

8. (V) _____

stick

9. (N) _____

10. (V) _____

smell

11. (N) _____

12. (V) _____

TASK 9: **Adjectives: Words That Describe Nouns and Pronouns**

Student Mastery Score	Minimum Mastery Score	Maximum Mastery Score
	17	21
80% or more correct, progress to next Task.		

Words used to describe nouns or pronouns are called adjectives. List as many adjectives as you can in each of the following categories. You may want to use a dictionary or thesaurus.

Colors   Shapes   Sizes

_____   _____   _____

_____   _____   _____

_____   _____   _____

_____   _____   _____

_____   _____   _____

_____   _____   _____

Student Mastery Score	Minimum Mastery Score	Maximum Mastery Score
	3	4
80% or more correct, progress to next Task.		

TASK 10: **Definitions**

The word **stand** has many meanings. Use a thesaurus to find four words or phrases that mean the same thing as **stand**.

1._____   2._____

3._____   4._____

Student Mastery Score	Minimum Mastery Score	Maximum Mastery Score
	7	9
80% or more correct, progress to next Task.		

TASK 11: **Nouns and Verbs**

Are these words nouns (names of persons, places, or things)? Or are they verbs (action words)? Remember, some words can be used as both a noun and a verb. For the following write **N**, **V**, or **N+V**.

1. chip _____

2. wish _____

3. thank _____

4. chill _____

5. thing _____

6. call _____

7. wham _____

8. dish _____

9. fish _____

Student Mastery Score	Minimum Mastery Score	Maximum Mastery Score
	13	16
80% or more correct, progress to next Task.		

TASK 12: **Pronouncing and Writing Words Correctly**

Read each sentence pair. Remember, **-ed** signals past time. Be sure to pronounce **-s** and **-ed** endings clearly.

Brad stacks the bricks. He stacked the bricks.

Ann smells the crabs. She smelled the crabs.

The bird flaps its wings. The bird flapped its wings.

Bill crashes his little cars. Bill crashed his little cars.

The ship docks at ten. It docked at ten.

She dashes off to work. She dashed off to work.

He ships the packages. He shipped the packages.

Tom whiffs the scent. Tom whiffed the scent.

Sam cashes his check. Sam cashed his check.

She tricks her friend. She tricked her friend.

Your teacher will read a sentence, then repeat one word. Write the word your teacher repeats. Decide whether or not each word needs an **-s** or **-ed** ending.

1. _____

2. _____

3. _____

4. _____

5. _____

6. _____

7. _____

8. _____

9. _____

10. _____

11. _____

12. _____

13. _____

14. _____

15. _____

16. _____

Student Mastery Score	Minimum Mastery Score	Maximum Mastery Score
	8	10
80% or more correct, progress to next Task.		

TASK 13: **Suffixes**

We will read each of the following sentences aloud. Think about the correct suffix for the word in each one. Then, write the correct word in the blank. Remember:

Add **-'s** to mean singular ownership.

Add **-s'** to mean plural ownership.

Add **-s** or **-es** to mean more than one (plural).

Add **-ing** to mean present time.

Add **-ed** to mean past time.

1. This (crab's, crabs') _____ back legs are missing.

2. The (twin's, twins') _____ dad packed their snacks in the boxes.

3. He stacked the flat red (bricks, brick's) _____ .

4. Are they (crossing, crossed) _____ the tracks?

5. They had fresh (drinks, drink's) _____ for the kids on the trip.

6. (Pat's, Pats') _____ stiff leg kept her from running.

7. Sid got up the (spills, spill's) _____ from the drinks.

8. Granddad said, "Put your glad (rags, rag's) _____ on!"

9. Your (trips, trip's) _____ plans are fantastic!

10. Nick (spilled, spilling) _____ the hot drinks on the carpet.

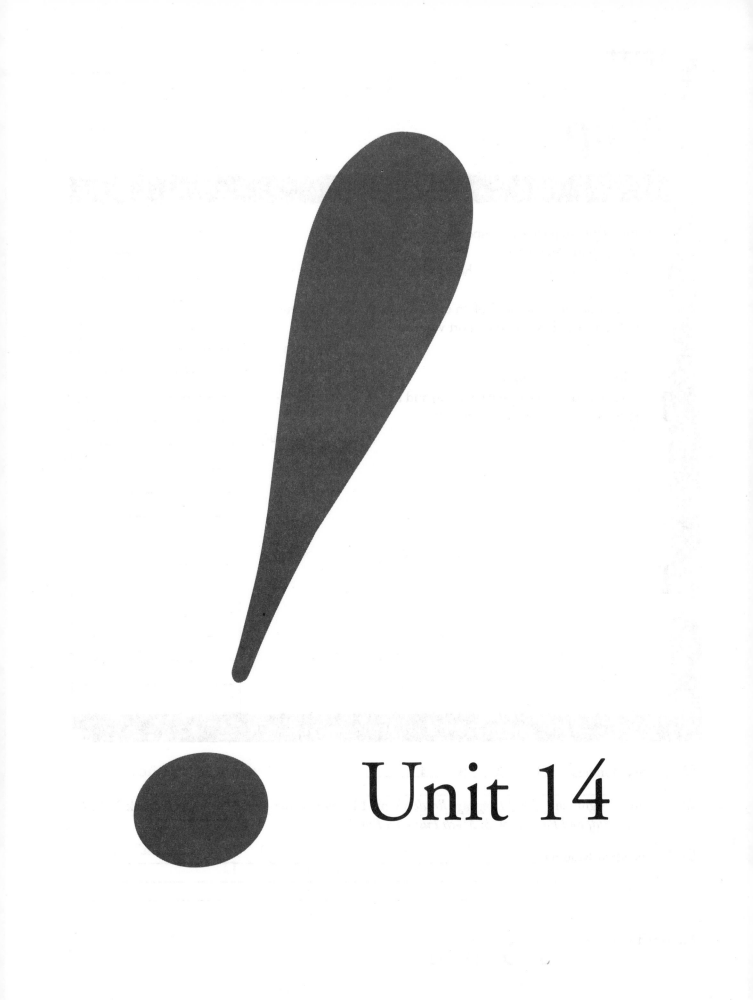

Unit 14

Instructional Content

WORDS TO READ/SPELL

-ush	-ud	-ug	-unk	-ung	-ub	-uff	-uck	-unch	Nonphonetic Words
blush	Bud	bugs	bunk	Chung	hub	huff	luck	Grunch	*too*
crush	mud	hug	chunks	flung	rub	puff	stuck	hunch	*Mr.*
rush				stung	shrub	stuff	truck	lunch	*Ms.*
					tub			munch	*Mrs.*

EXPANDED WORD LIST

bluff	drum	glut	plum	shrunk	smug	spud	stun
brush	flub	grub	plus	skull	snub	spun	trunk
club	fluff	gruff	scum	skunk	snuck	spunk	
cluck	flunk	pluck	shrub	slug	snuff	stub	
drug	glum	plug	shrug	slum	snug	stud	

FIVE FAVORITE IDIOMS OR EXPRESSIONS

1. _____

2. _____

3. _____

4. _____

5. _____

Tasks for Mastery

READING

Student Mastery Score	Minimum Mastery Score	Maximum Mastery Score
	58	72
80% or more correct, progress to next Task.		

TASK 1: **Phoneme Segmentation**

A. Each of the following words contains a consonant pair or a digraph. Some words have both. A **consonant pair** has two letters that represent the same consonant sound. A **digraph** is two consonant letters that represent a single unique sound. In the words that follow, circle each digraph. Underline each letter pair. (Do not mark blends.)

B. Say each word aloud. In the blank beside each word, write 3, 4, or 5 to tell how many different sounds you hear in each word.

1. Grunch ____ 2. hunch ____ 3. munch ____

4. lunch ____ 5. chunk ____ 6. thump ____

7. crush ____ 8. blush ____ 9. rush ____

10. hush ____ 11. much ____ 12. such ____

13. stuck ____ 14. luck ____ 15. which ____

16. them ____ 17. ships ____ 18. wish ____

19. wham ____ 20. thin ____ 21. dish ____

22. bath ____ 23. shock ____ 24. whiff ____

25. jazz ____ 26. pinch ____ 27. fish ____

28. wham ____ 29. Chick ____ 30. Thad ____

31. chuck ____ 32. thin ____ 33. than ____

34. dull ____ 35. stuff ____ 36. chunk ____

ENGLISH/LANGUAGE ARTS

Student Mastery Score	Minimum Mastery Score	Maximum Mastery Score
	10	12
80% or more correct, progress to next Task.		

TASK 6: Using Adjectives, the Describing Words

Adjectives are special words that tell more about nouns. Adjectives tell **which**, **what kind of**, or **how many**. Words like **tall**, **several**, and **beautiful** are adjectives. They can describe nouns.

In the following chart, words are listed as nouns, verbs, and adjectives. Use words from the lists and other words, too. Write the best sentences you can. (You may add endings to words and use extra words.)

Adjectives	Nouns	Verbs
dull	lunch	rush
much	bug	help
flat	shrubs	jump
brisk	truck	flung
fresh	bus	crash
black	clock	shrank
that	luck	chugs

1. _____
2. _____
3. _____
4. _____
5. _____
6. _____
7. _____
8. _____
9. _____
10. _____
11. _____
12. _____

Student Mastery Score	Minimum Mastery Score	Maximum Mastery Score
	10	12
80% or more correct, progress to next Task.		

TASK 7: **Reviewing Subjects**

In each sentence you wrote in Task 6, circle the word that is the subject. Remember, a subject names a person, place, thing, or idea that the sentence tells about.

Student Mastery Score	Minimum Mastery Score	Maximum Mastery Score
	8	10
80% or more correct, progress to next Task.		

TASK 8: **Morphology**

We will read each of the following sentences aloud. Think about the correct suffix for the word in each one. Then, write the correct word in the blank. Remember:

Add **-er** to an adjective to mean **more** (comparative).

Add **-est** to an adjective to mean the **most** (superlative).

Some questions have review suffixes.

1. That was the (duller, dullest) _____ class we had.

2. Are these chips (fresher, freshest) _____ than yours?

3. Could this be the (wetter, wettest) _____ dog at the vet's?

4. Pat said, "This is the (thinner, thinnest) _____ I can slice it."

5. Sis has the (thicker, thickest) _____ blanket we have.

6. Al can do the long (jump, jump's) _____ in track.

7. Sam (rubbed, rubbing) _____ the leg that got stung by the bugs.

8. Mrs. Chung (rushed, rushing) _____ to help the kids on the bus.

9. The hub (caps, cap's) _____ are missing from the van.

10. Sid and Tom are (munched, munching) _____ on the sandwiches.

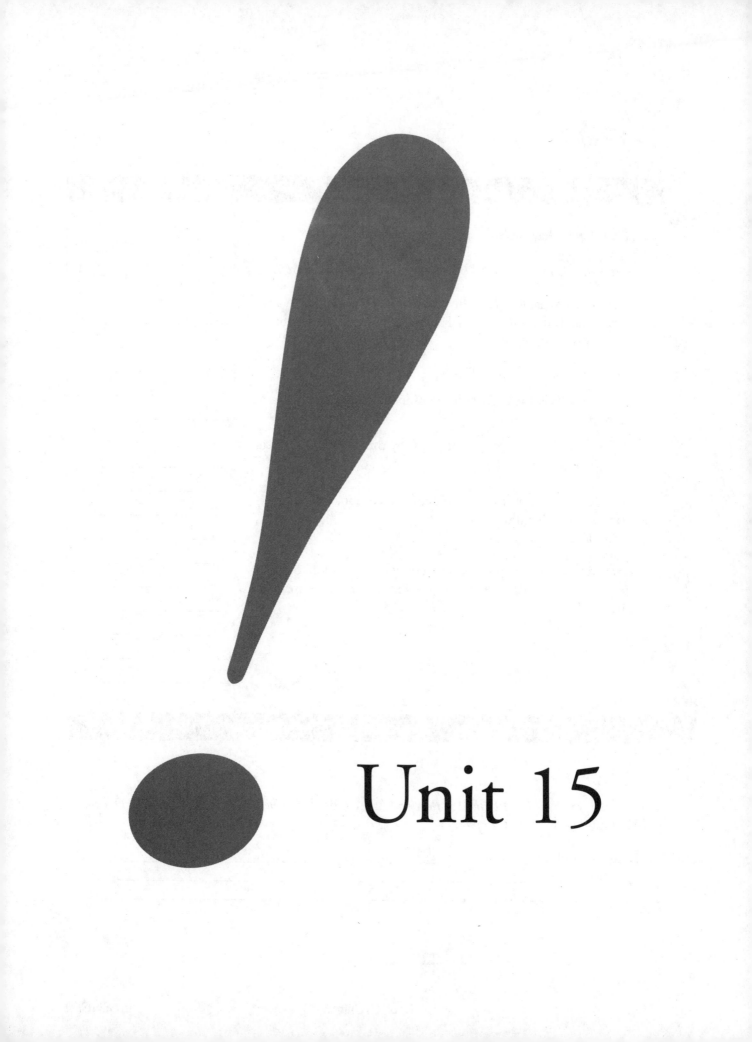

Unit 15

Map

CONCEPTS & CONTENT	NOTES & EXAMPLES

READING

SPELLING

❑ A word must have at least one vowel phoneme.

❑ Some vowels in unaccented syllables reduce to the **schwa** /ə/.

❑ Words have syllable parts. The number of vowel sounds in a word always equals the number of syllables in a word. Each syllable contains one vowel sound.

❑ A word has one or more syllables.

A **closed syllable** ends with a consonant phoneme and has a short vowel sound.

The sound for the vowel is signaled by the use of a diacritical mark, breve (˘).

❑ When two closed syllables are joined, two consonants that are next to each other often result.
Example: <u>bas</u> + <u>ket</u> = ba<u>sk</u>et

❑ **Analysis** questions require breaking down information. Some specific words signal an Analysis question: **arrange**, **compare**, **distinguish**.

ACTIVITIES, ASSIGNMENTS & ASSESSMENT

❑ Fluency Builders   1   2   3   4

❑ Reading Assignment: *J & J Language Readers* Unit 15, Book 1: *The Velvet Jacket*; Book 2: *Talcum and Twins*; Book 3: *At the Campus*

❑ Independent Reading: _____
_____
_____

Mastery Tasks   1   2   3   4   5
                     ❑   ❑   ❑   ❑   ❑

CONCEPTS & CONTENT	NOTES & EXAMPLES

❑ Quotation marks are used to set off direct quotations.

❑ Six Traits of Effective Writing:
Focus: Word Choice—Description

❑ Some verbs are not action words:
- Forms of **be** are verbs. Some forms of **be** are: **am**, **are**, **is**, **was**, **were**.
- Main verbs or helping verbs: Forms of **be** can be used as the main verb in a sentence. Forms of **be** can also be used as a helping verb in a sentence. Examples: am going, are sitting, is pulling, was fixing, were hopping

❑ A verb or verb phrase forms the **base predicate**.

❑ A verb may be the **main verb** or a **helping verb**.

❑ Correct forms of **be** are determined by:
- Number (singular or plural)
- Person (first = speaker; second = person spoken to; third = person spoken about)

	Singular	Plural
First Person	I **am**	we **are**
Second Person	you **are**	you **are**
Third Person	he, she, it **is**	they **are**

❑ Masterpiece Sentence
Focus: Stage 5: Paint Your Words
Precise words create a clearer description.

WRITING & ENGLISH LANGUAGE ARTS

ACTIVITIES, ASSIGNMENTS & ASSESSMENT

❑ Composition Assignment: _____

_____

_____

Mastery Tasks   6   7   8   9   10   11   12
                 ❑   ❑   ❑   ❑   ❑   ❑   ❑

Instructional Content

WORDS TO READ/SPELL

						Nonphonetic Word
admit	catnap	insect	picnic	shamrock	upset	*into*
basket	comic	jacket	pigpen	splendid	velvet	
backpack	fabric	locket	plastic	sunset	zigzag	
cactus	fantastic	muffin	pockets	talcum		
campus	frogman	napkin	rabbit	tickets		
cannot	goblin	padlock	ragbag	traffic		

EXPANDED WORD LIST

adding	clinic	discuss	enlist	frolic	mass transit
annex	complex	disestablish	enrich	gasket	medic
blacktop	compress	disinfect	entrap	hamlet	medical
blank check	conduct	dismiss	establish	inbred	misfit
blemish	conquest	dispel	express	inhabit	object
bran muffin	content	disrupt	finish	inherit	picket
cabin	contest	distill	flagship	instruct	pilgrim
candid	convict	dominant	flagstaff	intended	plexus
checklist	credit	dropkick	flapjacks	limit	pragmatic
clamshell	critic	droplet	flashback	magnet	public
classic	discredit	enact	frantic	mascot	

FIVE FAVORITE IDIOMS OR EXPRESSIONS

1. _____

2. _____

3. _____

4. _____

5. _____

Tasks for Mastery

READING

Student Mastery Score	Minimum Mastery Score	Maximum Mastery Score
	28	**35**
80% or more correct, progress to next Task.		

TASK 1: **Syllable Analysis**

A. Unit 15 words can be divided into word parts (syllables). Each syllable has one vowel (open) sound. Draw a line to divide each word into syllables. Underline letters that represent vowel sounds.

Examples: sun/set   plas/tic

1. velvet   2. splendid   3. napkin   4. cannot   5. padlock   6. insect

7. jacket   8. traffic   9. picnic   10. upset   11. locket   12. cactus

13. campus   14. zigzag   15. basket   16. ragbag   17. fantastic   18. tickets

19. comic   20. fabric   21. plastic   22. catnap   23. goblin   24. into

25. frogman   26. pockets   27. sunset   28. pigpen   29. rabbit   30. admit

31. muffin   32. fantastic   33. talcum   34. shamrock

B. Which Unit 15 word has three syllables?

_____

Student Mastery Score	Minimum Mastery Score	Maximum Mastery Score
	24	30
80% or more correct, progress to next Task.		

TASK 2: **Phoneme Segmentation**

Tell how many phonemes (single sounds) are in each of the Unit 15 words. Some sounds are represented by more than one letter. Be sure to listen for each separate sound you hear in each word. For example: s/p/l/e/n/d/i/d = 8.

1. velvet _____
2. splendid _____
3. napkin _____
4. cannot _____

5. padlock _____
6. jacket _____
7. traffic _____
8. picnic _____

9. upset _____
10. locket _____
11. campus _____
12. zigzag _____

13. basket _____
14. ragbag _____
15. fantastic _____
16. comic _____

17. fabric _____
18. plastic _____
19. catnap _____
20. goblin _____

21. frogman _____
22. pockets _____
23. sunset _____
24. pigpen _____

25. rabbit _____
26. admit _____
27. muffin _____
28. fantastic _____

29. talcum _____
30. shamrock _____

Student Mastery Score	Minimum Mastery Score	Maximum Mastery Score
	30	**37**
80% or more correct, progress to next Task.		

TASK 3: **Listening for Word Parts**

A. Phonemic Awareness
    Listen to each word. You will write part of each word. Your teacher will tell you which sound of the word to omit.

1. _____

2. _____

3. _____

4. _____

5. _____

6. _____

7. _____

8. _____

9. _____

10. _____

11. _____

12. _____

B. Listen to each word. Write the word part that your teacher repeats to you.

13._____ 14._____ 15._____ 16._____

17._____ 18._____ 19._____ 20._____

21._____ 22._____ 23._____ 24._____

25._____ 26._____ 27._____ 28._____

29._____ 30._____ 31._____ 32._____

33._____ 34._____ 35._____ 36._____

37._____

SPELLING

TASK 4: **Spelling Word List**

Student Mastery Score	Minimum Mastery Score	Maximum Mastery Score
	16	20
80% or more correct, progress to next Task.		

Write the words that your teacher dictates on the Spelling Practice forms in the back of this book.

TASK 5: **Spelling Mastery Sentences**

Student Mastery Score	Minimum Mastery Score	Maximum Mastery Score
	5	6
80% or more correct, progress to next Task.		

1. _____

   _____

2. _____

   _____

3. _____

   _____

4. _____

   _____

5. _____

   _____

6. _____

   _____

WRITING

TASK 6: **Quotation Marks, Punctuation, and Capitalization Review**

Student Mastery Score	Minimum Mastery Score	Maximum Mastery Score
	4	5
80% or more correct, progress to next Task.		

When we write what someone says, we put quotation marks before (") and after (") the words he or she says. Place quotation marks at the beginning and end of the words that are spoken in the following sentences. (When the words that are spoken begin in the middle of a sentence, the first word that is spoken begins with a capital. See sentences 1, 4, and 5.)

Circle letters that should be capitals in the following sentences. Put a period or question mark at the end of each sentence.

1. mom said, you can have a hot bran muffin on a napkin

2. would you kids get into pigpen slop if you could dad asked

3. i have to admit, dad said, you are fantastic

4. frogman fred said, the campus snack shop is the hot spot

5. pat said, did the kids dress up

ENGLISH/LANGUAGE ARTS

TASK 7: **Forms of Be as Helping Verbs Build Verb Phrases**

Student Mastery Score	Minimum Mastery Score	Maximum Mastery Score
	8	10
80% or more correct, progress to next Task.		

In each of the following sentences, an action verb is the main verb. Helping verbs are also used in each sentence. A helping verb combines with the main verb to create a verb phrase in the predicate. Helping verbs do not describe action. Verbs such as: **am**, **are**, **is**, **was**, and **were** (forms of the verb **be**) are verbs that can be used as helping verbs. They combine with main verbs to form a verb phrase.

Underline the verb phrase in each of the following sentences.

Examples:

I <u>am coming</u> with you.

We <u>were singing</u>.

Ted <u>is fixing</u> the ship.

Bill <u>was hit</u> with a ball.

1. I am drinking pop.

2. You are helping them win.

3. Ken Bell is planning the trip.

4. Jen was honking at him.

5. Sid and Mat are snacking on pizza.

6. Miss Pitman is quizzing the class.

7. Max and Al are dragging the tent into the yard.

8. Kim, Bud, Sid, and Sam were wishing that math would end.

9. Rick was fishing with us.

10. Pam is fixing lunch for the kids.

Student Mastery Score	Minimum Mastery Score	Maximum Mastery Score
	16	20
80% or more correct, progress to next Task.		

TASK 8: **Words and Meanings**

Use a thesaurus to find two other words that mean the same as each of the following words.

1. admit   _____ _____

2. basket   _____ _____

3. goblin   _____ _____

4. fantastic   _____ _____

5. upset   _____ _____

6. insect   _____ _____

7. ask   _____ _____

8. jacket   _____ _____

9. splendid   _____ _____

10. fabric   _____ _____

Student Mastery Score	Minimum Mastery Score	Maximum Mastery Score
	11	14
80% or more correct, progress to next Task.		

TASK 9: **More About Adjectives**

The following words can be used as adjectives. Write a sentence using each of these words as an adjective. Remember, adjectives describe nouns or pronouns. Adjectives tell which, what kind of, and how many.

1. velvet _____

2. fantastic _____

3. plastic _____

4. comic _____

5. talcum _____

6. dull _____

7. much _____

8. rusted _____

9. flat _____

10. fresh _____

11. black _____

12. slim _____

13. cross _____

14. red _____

Student Mastery Score	Minimum Mastery Score	Maximum Mastery Score
	6	8
80% or more correct, progress to next Task.		

TASK 10: **Verbs That Are Not Action Verbs**

Some verbs are not action words. In the following list, circle the verbs that do not describe action.

was	hit	are	lick	kick	have
is	hack	bit	had	fix	fell
beg	bet	had	were	put	am

Student Mastery Score	Minimum Mastery Score	Maximum Mastery Score
	11	14
80% or more correct, progress to next Task.		

TASK 11: **Verbs May Be Main Verbs or Helping Verbs**

A. A verb may be a main verb or a helping verb. The helping verb form of **be** can be used with a main verb in the predicate. A helping verb does not describe action but can be used as the main verb in the predicate. Refer to the verbs in the previous exercise and complete the following:

1. List at least five words that can be used as main verbs to describe action.

_____   _____   _____

_____   _____

2. List at least three words that are helping verbs.

_____   _____   _____

3. List at least three words that can be used as both helping verbs and main verbs and are not action verbs.

_____   _____   _____

B. Choose one verb from each of the three lists you identified in the previous activity. Write three sentences using each predicate verb in the verb form as it was specified in the lists above (as a main verb, a helping verb + a main verb, and a helping verb that acts as a main verb).

4. _____

_____

5. _____

_____

6. _____

_____

Student Mastery Score	Minimum Mastery Score	Maximum Mastery Score
	8	10
80% or more correct, progress to next Task.		

TASK 12: **Suffixes**

We will read each of the following sentences aloud. Think about the correct suffix for the word in each one. Then, write the correct word in the blank. Remember:

Add **-er** to an adjective to mean **more** (comparative).

Add **-est** to an adjective to mean **most** (superlative).

Some questions have review suffixes.

1. The (baskets, basket's) _____ are filled with snacks.

2. She (admitted, admitting) _____ that she put the locket into his jacket

   pocket.

3. It is your turn; they (fixed, fixing) _____ the last picnic.

4. I cannot help him if he (stops, stop's) _____ helping himself.

5. Did Tom have (padlocks, padlock's) _____ ?

6. The four (fresher, freshest) _____ muffins are in the basket.

7. The two traffic (cop's, cops') _____ skills got us back.

8. Tam said, "This kitten is (softer, softest) _____ than that kitten."

9. Sunsets of red, pink, and orange got (softer, softest) _____ as the sun

   dropped.

10. Al got (ticketed, ticketing) _____ for reckless driving.

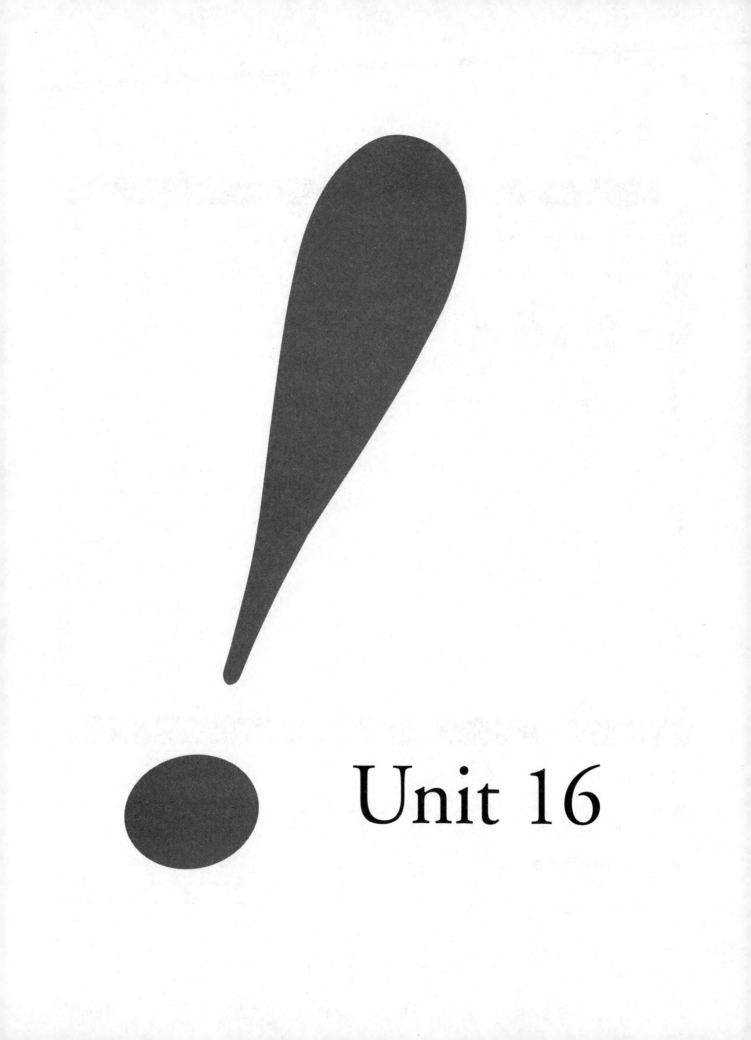

Unit 16

Map

CONCEPTS & CONTENT	NOTES & EXAMPLES

READING

❑ Consonant combinations (**clusters**) in this unit: /str/, /spr/, /spl/, /scr/

In a consonant cluster, all three phonemes are heard.

❑ The most complex syllables in English contain three adjacent consonants.

Awareness of all three consonants sounds is necessary to spell accurately.

All of the three consonant clusters begin with <u>s</u>.

SPELLING

ACTIVITIES, ASSIGNMENTS & ASSESSMENT

❑ Fluency Builders   1   2   3   4

❑ Reading Assignment: *J & J Language Readers* Unit 16, Book 1: *The Spring Picnic*; Book 2: *Scram!*; Book 3: *A Big Splash*

❑ Independent Reading: _____

_____

_____

Mastery Tasks   1   2   3   4   5   6   7
                   ❑   ❑   ❑   ❑   ❑   ❑   ❑

CONCEPTS & CONTENT	NOTES & EXAMPLES

WRITING ~ ENGLISH LANGUAGE ARTS

❑ Six Traits of Effective Writing:
Focus: Word Choice—descriptive adjectives and details

❑ A complete sentence has a predicate component.

❑ A verb or verb phrase forms the base predicate: The base predicate has a main verb that tells what the subject does or is. The main verb of the base predicate can be an action verb.

❑ More helping verbs: Forms of **have** may be used as helping verbs. Examples: have jumped, has put, had sat

❑ Words that are helping verbs can also be used as main verbs: A form of **be** or a form of **have** can be the main verb or a helping verb.

❑ Verbs: **past participle**: <u>-en</u>, (got, gotten); <u>-ed</u>, (earn, earned)

❑ Masterpiece Sentence
Focus: Stage 5: Paint Your Words

ACTIVITIES, ASSIGNMENTS & ASSESSMENT

❑ Composition Assignment: _____
_____
_____

Mastery Tasks   8   9   10   11   12   13
                     ❑   ❑   ❑   ❑   ❑   ❑

Instructional Content

WORDS TO READ/SPELL

str	spr	spl	scr	Other	Nonphonetic Word
strap	sprang	splash	scram	Scott	*were*
stress	spring	splat	scraps		
strict	sprung	split	scrub		
strum					
strip					
strong					
strum					
strung					

EXPANDED WORD LIST

construct	splint	sprat	stratus	stripped
scrim	split ticket	sprig	strength	stripping
scrimp	split second	sprint	strengthen	strongbox
script	split shift	sprocket	stressful	struck
scrunch	split-level	strand	stricken	strut
splendid	splotch	stranded	strictest	

FIVE FAVORITE IDIOMS OR EXPRESSIONS

1. _____

2. _____

3. _____

4. _____

5. _____

Tasks for Mastery

READING

Student Mastery Score	Minimum Mastery Score	Maximum Mastery Score
	10	**12**
80% or more correct, progress to next Task.		

TASK 1: Phoneme Segmentation

Place a mark (·) above each separate phoneme in the following consonant clusters. As you make each mark, say each separate sound aloud. Then blend the sounds.

Example: s͘p͘l͘ash

1. spring   2. street   3. sprung   4. string   5. scram   6. split

7. stress   8. strip   9. sprang   10. strong   11. strap   12. splash

Student Mastery Score	Minimum Mastery Score	Maximum Mastery Score
	29	36
80% or more correct, progress to next Task.		

TASK 2: **Listening for Word Parts**

A. Listen to each word. Write the word part that your teacher repeats to you.

1. _____   2. _____   3. _____

4. _____   5. _____   6. _____

7. _____   8. _____   9. _____

10. _____   11. _____   12. _____

13. _____   14. _____   15. _____

16. _____   17. _____   18. _____

19. _____   20. _____   21. _____

22. _____   23. _____   24. _____

25. _____

B. Phonemic Awareness
   Listen to each word. You will write part of each word. Your teacher will tell you which sounds to omit.

26. _____

27. _____

28. _____

29. _____

30. _____

31. _____

32. _____

33. _____

34. _____

35. _____

36. _____

Student Mastery Score	Minimum Mastery Score	Maximum Mastery Score
	24	30
80% or more correct, progress to next Task.		

TASK 3: **Listening for Initial Blends and Clusters**

Listen to the following words and write the initial blend or cluster you hear. As you write each blend, pronounce it aloud.

1._____ 2._____ 3._____ 4._____ 5._____ 6._____

7._____ 8._____ 9._____ 10._____ 11._____ 12._____

13._____ 14._____ 15._____ 16._____ 17._____ 18._____

19._____ 20._____ 21._____ 22._____ 23._____ 24._____

25._____ 26._____ 27._____ 28._____ 29._____ 30._____

Student Mastery Score	Minimum Mastery Score	Maximum Mastery Score
	14	17
80% or more correct, progress to next Task.		

TASK 4: **Consonant Clusters**

Practice writing the "consonant cluster" words from the Unit 16 vocabulary in the following blanks. As you write each of the initial consonant clusters, pronounce all three of the sounds aloud.

1. _____   2. _____

3. _____   4. _____

5. _____   6. _____

7. _____   8. _____

9. _____   10. _____

11. _____   12. _____

13. _____   14. _____

15. _____   16. _____

17. _____

SPELLING

Student Mastery Score	Minimum Mastery Score	Maximum Mastery Score
	13	16
80% or more correct, progress to next Task.		

TASK 5: **More Initial Consonant Clusters**

Use the dictionary to find four new English words that begin with each of these Unit 16 initial consonant clusters.

str-	**spr-**	**spl-**	**scr-**
_____	_____	_____	_____
_____	_____	_____	_____
_____	_____	_____	_____
_____	_____	_____	_____

Student Mastery Score	Minimum Mastery Score	Maximum Mastery Score
	17	21
80% or more correct, progress to next Task.		

TASK 6: **Spelling Word List**

Write the words that your teacher dictates on the Spelling Practice forms in the back of this book.

Student Mastery Score	Minimum Mastery Score	Maximum Mastery Score
	6	7
80% or more correct, progress to next Task.		

TASK 7: Spelling Mastery Sentences

1. _____

   _____

2. _____

   _____

3. _____

   _____

4. _____

   _____

5. _____

   _____

6. _____

   _____

7. _____

   _____

ENGLISH/LANGUAGE ARTS

TASK 8: **Forms of Have as Helping Verbs Build Verb Phrases**

Student Mastery Score	Minimum Mastery Score	Maximum Mastery Score
	8	10
80% or more correct, progress to next Task.		

In each of the following sentences, an action verb is the main verb. Helping verbs can combine with the main verb to create a verb phrase in the predicate. Helping verbs do not describe action.

Review: Forms of **be** (**am, are, is, was, were**) can be used as helping verbs. Forms of **have** (**has, had, have**) can also be used as helping verbs. Helping verbs combine with the main verb to form a verb **phrase.**

Underline the verb phrase in each of the following sentences.

Examples:

　　I <u>had called</u> for you.

　　We <u>have wished</u> to win.

　　Ted <u>has fixed</u> the ship.

　　You <u>had met</u> Bill.

1. I had snacked on pizza.

2. You have let them win.

3. Ken Wattling had planned the trip.

4. Rod and the man have honked at us.

5. Mick and Nat had dragged the bats and balls.

6. Miss Pitt has quizzed the class.

7. Max and Mel have dragged the tent into the yard.

8. Tim, Tom, and Dan have wished that class would end.

9. Rick has got the lunch for us in his truck.

10. Dad has fixed lunch for the kids.

Student Mastery Score	Minimum Mastery Score	Maximum Mastery Score
	16	20
80% or more correct, progress to next Task.		

TASK 9: **Learning About Words**

Use a thesaurus to find two other words that mean the same as each of the following words.

1. spring _____ _____

2. strap _____ _____

3. strong _____ _____

4. stress _____ _____

5. strict _____ _____

6. street _____ _____

7. strip _____ _____

8. splash _____ _____

9. splendid _____ _____

10. split _____ _____

Student Mastery Score	Minimum Mastery Score	Maximum Mastery Score
	24	30
80% or more correct, progress to next Task.		

TASK 10: **A Verb or Verb Phrase as the Base Predicate**

In each of the following sentences, the action verb is the main verb in the predicate that tells what the subject does or is. Helping verbs (such as forms of **be: am**, **is**, **are**, **was**, and **were**, or **have: has**, **had**, and **have**) can also combine with the main verb to form a verb phrase in the base predicate. Helping verbs do not describe action but can be used as the main verb in a sentence.

A. Using the words in the box, fill in the blanks with the verb or verb phrase that best completes each sentence.

1. Ted _____ _____ a plastic lid on the grass.

2. We _____ a string on the red basket.

3. "I _____ the rich king of the hill!" yelled Jack.

4. They _____ a big bash at sunset.

5. Dad _____ the fat bug on his leg.

6. She _____ _____ at the jazz picnic.

7. The big cat _____ _____ from the tree.

8. The birds _____ _____ in our back yard.

9. Scott _____ _____ the ham.

10. The traffic _____ bad on campus.

have	has	had	am	is
was	were	kicking	chirping	chill
grilling	crushed	bugs	sprung	singing
yell	slash	strung	brisk	bad
big	are			

B. Place an **H** above the word(s) in each sentence that is the helping verb (forms of **be**: **am**, **is**, **are**, **was**, and **were**, or **have**: **has**, **had**, and **have**) and an **M** above the word that is the main verb.

TASK 11: **Reviewing Forms of Be as Helping Verbs**

Student Mastery Score	Minimum Mastery Score	Maximum Mastery Score
	4	5
80% or more correct, progress to next Task.		

Refer to the previous task and select those sentences in which a form of **be** (**am**, **is**, **are**, **was**, and **were**) is used as a helping verb. Write each sentence number in the spaces here. Rewrite each sentence using a different form of **be** to complete the sentence.

Examples: Nell was tossing the stack of sticks.
Nell is tossing the stack of sticks.

Sentence #

_____   _____

_____   _____

_____   _____

_____   _____

_____   _____

Student Mastery Score	Minimum Mastery Score	Maximum Mastery Score
	8	10
80% or more correct, progress to next Task.		

TASK 12: **Reviewing Adjectives**

Adjectives describe nouns or pronouns and tell **which**, **what kind of**, and **how many**. Go back and circle the adjectives in the sentences from Task 10.

Student Mastery Score	Minimum Mastery Score	Maximum Mastery Score
	8	10
80% or more correct, progress to next Task.		

TASK 13: **Suffixes**

Read each of the following sentences aloud. Then, write the correct word in each blank. Remember, participle verb forms are used with helping verbs. Add **-ed** or **-en** to a verb that follows **had** or **have**.

Some questions contain review suffixes.

1. They had (gotten, gotting) _____ into the hot tub.

2. Sam and Sid have (boxed, boxes) _____ the lunches for the picnic.

3. The taxi has (honk, honked) _____ at them to get off the street.

4. They had (fish, fished) _____ in that pond.

5. Have you (thank, thanked) _____ Miss Pitt?

6. The class had (conduct, conducted) _____ the test at the campus.

7. They had (object, objected) _____ to the class.

8. The band had (stun, stunned) _____ us with their talent.

9. The (shrubs, shrub's) _____ prickly branch scratched my hand.

10. (Critic's, Critics) _____ had said this band was fantastic.

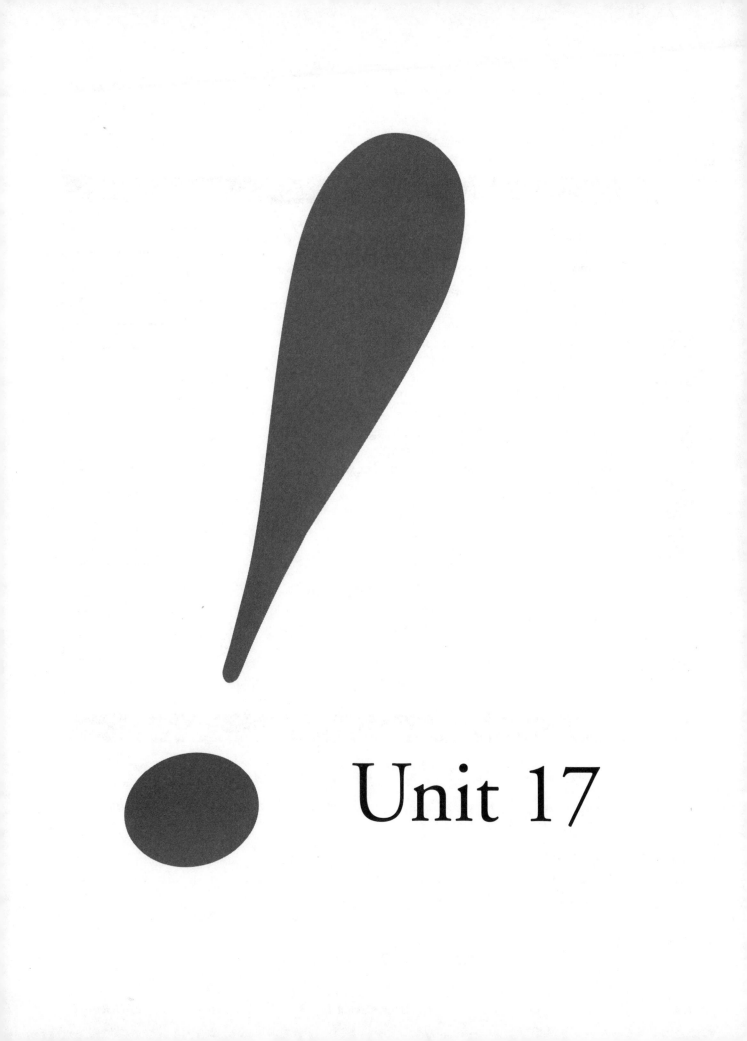

Unit 17

Map

CONCEPTS & CONTENT	NOTES & EXAMPLES

❑ Two or three consonants may occur after a vowel in a syllable.

❑ Phoneme-grapheme correspondences in this unit: **-st**, **-sk**, **-sp**, **-nt**, **-mp**, **-nd**, **-ld**, **-lk**, **-ft**, **-lp**, **-lt**, **-pt**, **-ct**
Letter pairs that represent two different consonant phonemes at the end of a word are called final blends.
Both consonant sounds are heard in **final blends**.

❑ **Homophones** are words that sound alike but are spelled differently and have different meanings. Examples: to, too, two. (Mnemonic [memory] cues can assist storage and retrieval of words that are easily confused. For example, "two, twenty, twelve" helps signal the **w** in two, the number word.)

READING ~ SPELLING

ACTIVITIES, ASSIGNMENTS & ASSESSMENT

❑ Fluency Builders   1   2   3   4

❑ Reading Assignment: *J & J Language Readers* Unit 17, Book 1: *Pumpkins, Masks, and Goblins*; Book 2: *At Camp*; Book 3: *The Land Fill*

❑ Independent Reading: _____
_____

Mastery Tasks   1   2   3   4   5
                       ❑   ❑   ❑   ❑   ❑

CONCEPTS & CONTENT	NOTES & EXAMPLES

❑ Six Traits of Effective Writing:
Focus:
  • Word Choice
  • Voice
 	
❑ Masterpiece Sentence
Focus: Stage 5: Paint Your Words	

WRITING & ENGLISH LANGUAGE ARTS

ACTIVITIES, ASSIGNMENTS & ASSESSMENT

❑ Composition Assignment: _____

_____

_____

Mastery Tasks
6	7	8	9	10	11	12	13	14	15
❑	❑	❑	❑	❑	❑	❑	❑	❑	❑

Instructional Content

WORDS TO READ/SPELL

-mp	-sk	-nt	-st	-ft	-nd	Other	Nonphonetic Words
clumps	ask	dent	best	drift	blond	act	*any*
pump	dusk	mint	frost	soft	grand	grasp	*do*
stump	mask		last			kilt	*many*
			trust			silk	*two*
						trick 'r treat	

EXPANDED WORD LIST

-st words

accompanist	bust	cost	eldest	glummest	mast
activist	capitalist	crest	encrust	gust	Midwest
adjusted	cast	crispest	enlist	hottest	mist
assist	checklist	crust	entrust	inquest	modest
attest	chest	dampest	exist	invest	must
bedfast	colonist	dentist	fast	jest	nest
biggest	columnist	dimmest	fastest	just	oddest
blacklist	conquest	disgust	fist	limpest	past
blast	consist	distrust	flabbergast	list	pest
blondest	contest	druggist	fondest	lushest	plumpest
bluntest	contested	dullest	gabfest	maddest	plushest
bombastic	contrast	dust	gladdest	manifest	poshest

-sk words

bask	damask	disk	frisk	husk	mollusk
brisk	desk	flask	gas mask	magnetic disk	musk

-sp words

asp	crisp	handclasp	lisp	unclasp
clasp	gasp	hospital	rasp	wisp

-nt words

absent	chant	consultant	embellishment	grant	pants
accomplishment	clement	content	eminent	grunt	penchant
advent	Clint	contentment	enactment	hint	pendant
allotment	cognizant	contestant	enhance	hunt	pent
annulment	combatant	continent	enchantment	imminent	plant
applicant	commandment	convent	establishment	implant	pregnant
assessment	commencement	detriment	expectant	imprint	present
assistant	comment	diminishment	experiment	indignant	prevalent
astonishment	commitment	dint	extent	infant	print
attachment	compliment	disenchant	figment	intent	prominent
attendant	concomitant	dissent	flint	invent	
banishment	condiment	dissident	flippant	investment	
bent	consent	distant	font	lent	
blunt	consistent	dominant	fulfillment	lint	
brunt	consonant	element	gallant	misprint	
bunt	constant	embankment	glint	pant	

-mp words

amp	chimp	cramp	hump	plump	rump
blimp	chomp	crimp	jump	pomp	scamp
bump	chump	damp	lamp	primp	scrimp
camp	clamp	dump	limp	ramp	shrimp
champ	clump	grump	lump	romp	skimp

-nd words

addend	cabstand	England	fund	impending	mend
amend	command	expand	gangland	inkstand	millpond
and	commend	expend	gland	inland	misspend
backhand	contend	extend	grandstand	intend	offend
bandstand	cropland	farmhand	grassland	kickstand	offhand
bend	deckhand	farmland	Greenland	land	pond
bland	disband	fend	hand	Lapland	quicksand
blend	distend	flatland	handstand	left-handed	ranchland
bond	dockhand	fond	hatband	lend	recommend
brand	end	frond	Holland	longhand	sand

-ld words

gild	handheld	held	meld	upheld	veld

-lk words

bulk	elk	hulk	milk	skim milk	sulk

-ft words

aft	draft	left	rift	sift	stick shift
cleft	gift	lift	shaft	skin graft	swift
craft	graft	loft	shift	spendthrift	theft
crankshaft	handcraft	raft	shoplift	split shift	thrift

-lp words

alp	gulp	help	pulp	scalp	self-help

-lt words

belt	cult	exult	insult	lilt	quilt
black belt	difficult	felt	jilt	melt	smelt
consult	dwelt	hilt	jolt	pelt	spilt

-pt words

attempt	contempt	exempt	prompt	sculpt	swept
bankrupt	crept	inept	rapt	slept	tempt
conscript	disrupt	kept	script	subscript	transcript

-sp words

clasp	crisp	grasp	lisp

-ct words

abduct	conduct	contradict	enact	induct	instinct
abstract	conflict	convict	exact	inexact	instruct
addict	conjunct	disconnect	expect	infect	intact
adjunct	connect	disinfect	extinct	inflect	intellect
affect	constrict	distinct	extract	inflict	matter-of-fact
aspect	construct	distract	fact	inject	misconduct
compact	contact	district	impact	insect	object
concoct	contract	duct	indistinct	inspect	obstruct

FIVE FAVORITE IDIOMS OR EXPRESSIONS

1. _____

2. _____

3. _____

4. _____

5. _____

Tasks for Mastery

READING

Student Mastery Score	Minimum Mastery Score	Maximum Mastery Score
	16	20
80% or more correct, progress to next Task.		

TASK 1: **Phoneme Segmentation**

Final blends are consonant letter combinations representing two or more different consonant phonemes at the end of a word. Place a mark (•) above each separate phoneme in the following final blends. As you make each mark, say each separate sound aloud. Then blend the sounds.

Example: fro̤st

1. frost	2. mint	3. trust	4. mask	5. pump
6. dusk	7. clump	8. silk	9. last	10. best
11. grasp	12. soft	13. act	14. stump	15. ask
16. blond	17. grand	18. dent	19. drift	20. kilt

Student Mastery Score	Minimum Mastery Score	Maximum Mastery Score
	30	**37**
80% or more correct, progress to next Task.		

TASK 2: **Listening for Word Parts**

A. Listen to each word. Write the word part that your teacher repeats to you.

1._____ 2._____ 3._____ 4._____

5._____ 6._____ 7._____ 8._____

9._____ 10._____ 11._____ 12._____

13._____ 14._____ 15._____ 16._____

17._____ 18._____ 19._____ 20._____

21._____ 22._____ 23._____ 24._____

25._____

B. Phonemic Awareness
    Listen to each word. You will write part of each word. Your teacher will tell you which
    word parts to omit.

26. _____

27. _____

28. _____

29. _____

30. _____

31. _____

32. _____

33. _____

34. _____

35. _____

36. _____

37. _____

Student Mastery Score	Minimum Mastery Score	Maximum Mastery Score
	16	20
80% or more correct, progress to next Task.		

TASK 3: **Phonemic Awareness**

Listen to the words and write the final blend you hear in the following blanks. As you write each blend, pronounce both of its sounds aloud.

1._____ 2._____ 3._____ 4._____ 5._____

6._____ 7._____ 8._____ 9._____ 10._____

11._____ 12._____ 13._____ 14._____ 15._____

16._____ 17._____ 18._____ 19._____ 20._____

SPELLING

Student Mastery Score	Minimum Mastery Score	Maximum Mastery Score
	17	21
80% or more correct, progress to next Task.		

TASK 4: **Spelling Word List**

Write the words that your teacher dictates on the Spelling Practice forms in the back of this book.

Student Mastery Score	Minimum Mastery Score	Maximum Mastery Score
	5	6
80% or more correct, progress to next Task.		

TASK 5: **Spelling Mastery Sentences**

1. _____

_____

2. _____

_____

3. _____

_____

4. _____

_____

5. _____

_____

6. _____

_____

WRITING

Student Mastery Score	Minimum Mastery Score	Maximum Mastery Score
	6	8
80% or more correct, progress to next Task.		

TASK 6: **Using Vocabulary**

Use each of the following Unit 17 vocabulary words to write a good sentence. Try adding prefixes or suffixes to the words.

1. trust _____

2. dusk _____

3. stump _____

4. blond _____

5. dent _____

6. many _____

7. pump _____

8. any _____

ENGLISH/LANGUAGE ARTS

TASK 7: **Forms of Do as Helping Verbs Build Verb Phrases**

Student Mastery Score	Minimum Mastery Score	Maximum Mastery Score
	7	9
80% or more correct, progress to next Task.		

In each of the following sentences, an action verb is the main verb. Helping verbs are also used in each sentence. A helping verb can combine with the main verb to create a verb phrase in the predicate. Helping verbs do not describe action.

Review: Forms of be (**am, are, is, was, were**); forms of **have** (**has, had, have**); and forms of **do** (**do, did, does**) can all be used as helping verbs. Helping verbs combine with the main verb to form a verb phrase.

Underline the verb phrase in the following sentences.
Examples:

I <u>do sing</u> with you.

We <u>did wish</u> to win.

Ted <u>does fix</u> the ship.

He <u>does help</u> Bill.

1. Tom did snack on the two pizzas.

2. You do help us with many swim meets.

3. Ken Strong does plan these grand trips.

4. Rod and the blond man did honk at us.

5. Scott and Nat did drag the bats and balls for many blocks.

6. Miss Storm does quiz the class.

7. Scott and Mel do put the tent up in the yard.

8. Tim, Tom, and Dan did wish that class would end.

9. Rick did get the dents bumped out of his truck.

Student Mastery Score	Minimum Mastery Score	Maximum Mastery Score
	16	20
80% or more correct, progress to next Task.		

TASK 8: **Learning About Words**

Use a thesaurus to find two other words that mean the same as the following words.

1. dusk _____ _____ 2. trust _____ _____

3. start _____ _____ 4. soft _____ _____

5. best _____ _____ 6. last _____ _____

7. grand _____ _____ 8. dent _____ _____

9. ask _____ _____ 10. act _____ _____

Student Mastery Score	Minimum Mastery Score	Maximum Mastery Score
	12	15
80% or more correct, progress to next Task.		

TASK 9: **Word Associations**

List as many Unit 17 words as you can associate with the following topics.

Halloween	**Camp**	**Landfill**

Student Mastery Score	Minimum Mastery Score	Maximum Mastery Score
	14	17
80% or more correct, progress to next Task.		

TASK 10: **Prefixes and Suffixes**

A. Add prefixes and suffixes to make new words from these Unit 17 words.

1. trust + ed _____

2. soft + er _____

3. frost +ing _____

4. re + start _____

5. de + frost + ed _____

6. start + ing _____

7. drift + er _____

8. dent + ing _____

9. stomp + ing _____

10. ask + ed _____

B. What new word from part A has a prefix and a suffix?

11. _____

C. In one new word, the suffix does not create a separate syllable. Which new word has only one vowel phoneme?

12. _____

D. Add **un-**, **re-**, and **de-** prefixes to make new words.

13. act   14. think   15. string   16. frost   17. start

_____   _____   _____   _____   _____

_____

Student Mastery Score	Minimum Mastery Score	Maximum Mastery Score
	16	20
80% or more correct, progress to next Task.		

TASK 11: **More Suffixes**

Add **-ing** and **-ed** endings to make new verbs from these Unit 17 words.

frost	**start**	**dent**	**ask**	**pump**
1._____	3._____	5._____	7._____	9._____
2._____	4._____	6._____	8._____	10._____

trust	**last**	**stump**	**act**	**mask**
11._____	13._____	15._____	17._____	19._____
12._____	14._____	16._____	18._____	20._____

TASK 12: **Reviewing Helping Verbs and Main Verbs**

Student Mastery Score	Minimum Mastery Score	Maximum Mastery Score
	8	10
80% or more correct, progress to next Task.		

Using an article or other passage of text, locate the verb or verb phrases in the predicates of at least ten sentences. Remember, the main verb in the predicate may be an action verb or a helping verb (**am**, **are**, **is**, **was**, **were**, **had**, **has**, **have**, **do**, **did**, **does**) that describes what the subject does or is. A verb phrase is a main verb combined with a helping verb. In the spaces here, write the sentence number and the verb or verb phrase you have identified (write **N/A** for helping verb if there is only a main verb).

Sentence Number	Helping Verb	Main Verb
1.		
2.		
3.		
4.		
5.		
6.		
7.		
8.		
9.		
10.		

Student Mastery Score	Minimum Mastery Score	Maximum Mastery Score
	4	5
80% or more correct, progress to next Task.		

TASK 13: **Helping Verbs as Main Verbs**

From your *J & J Language Reader* Unit 17 stories, identify five sentences in which at least one of each helping verb form (**be**, **have**, and **do**) is used as the main verb in the predicate. Write each sentence in the spaces here and circle the helping verb that is used as the main verb. Identify the page number on which the sentence appears and what form (**be**, **have**, or **do**) the verb represents.

Sentence   **Verb Form**   **Page**

1. _____   _____   _____

2. _____   _____   _____

3. _____   _____   _____

4. _____   _____   _____

5. _____   _____   _____

Student Mastery Score	Minimum Mastery Score	Maximum Mastery Score
	8	10
80% or more correct, progress to next Task.		

TASK 14: **Reviewing Verbs and Verb Phrases in the Predicate**

A. Following is an excerpt from Unit 17 Book 2: *At Camp*, in the *J & J Language Reader*. Write at least five sentences that describe what might happen next in the story. Use your imagination and creativity to convey a different outcome from the one presented in the actual story. You will only be responsible for spelling correctly those you have been taught.

At six, the camp bell rang. It was the mess bell, and the kids could not get to the camp mess too fast. But Tam said, "I think that is Pat!" "Ants! Ants!" Pat was yelling. "I have a hundred red ants in my…

1. _____

2. _____

3. _____

4. _____

5. _____

B. In the sentences you wrote for part A, circle the verb phrase. Above the main verb write **M** if it is the main verb, or **H** if it is a helping verb.

Student Mastery Score	Minimum Mastery Score	Maximum Mastery Score
	8	10
80% or more correct, progress to next Task.		

TASK 15: **Suffixes**

We will read each of the following sentences aloud. Think about the correct suffix for the word in each one. Then, write the correct word in the blank.

1. They had (adjust, adjusted) _____ to the class.

2. Kim has the (richer, richest) _____ singing voice in the class.

3. Sid had (acted, act) _____ in the class play.

4. The kids dressed up and had (masks, mask's) _____ for trick 'r treating.

5. Sis is (started, starting) _____ band lessons.

6. The raft had (drift, drifted) _____ from the dock.

7. This bed is (softer, softest) _____ than yours.

8. (Holland's, Hollands') _____ capital is Amsterdam.

9. They had (plan, planned) _____ a trip to Wisconsin.

10. The men had (pump, pumped) _____ the water from the swimming pool.

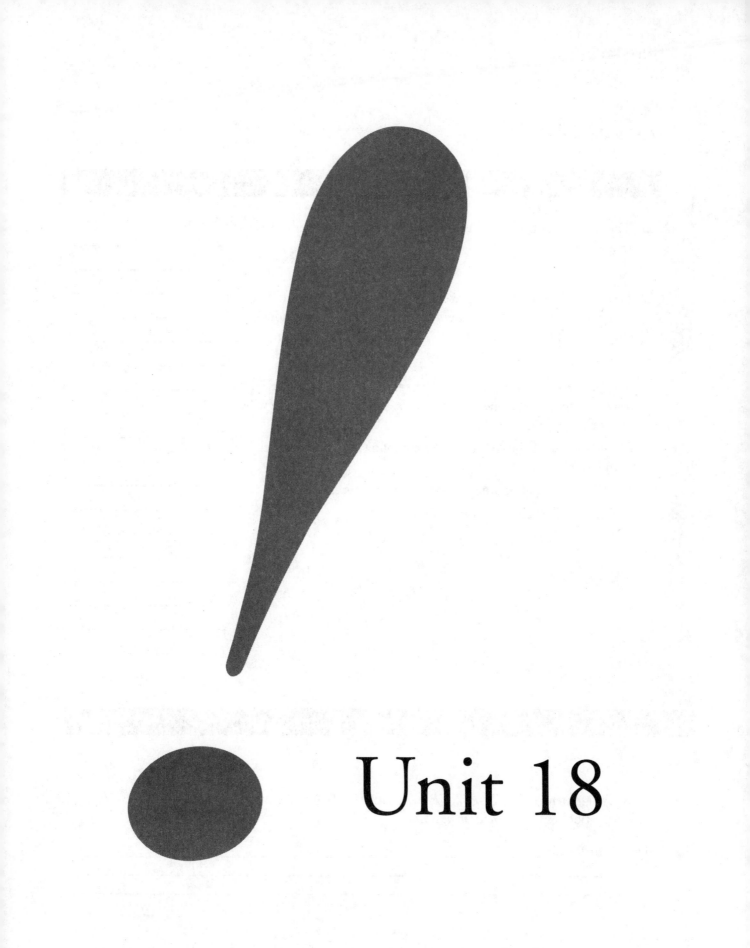

Unit 18

Map

CONCEPTS & CONTENT	NOTES & EXAMPLES

READING

❑ The number of phonemes is not the same as the number of letters in a word.

❑ Letter combinations can represent a single sound (phoneme). Some graphemes are three letters (e.g., **tch** for /*ch*/) even though they stand for one phoneme.

❑ The phoneme /*ch*/ is encoded with the letters **-tch** after short vowels at the ends of one-syllable words. The position of /*ch*/ will affect the spelling:

- /*ch*/ will usually be **-tch** immediately following a short vowel, as in **batch**.

- /*ch*/ will be **ch** after other phonemes, as in **bunch**.

- Exceptions: such, rich, much, which

SPELLING

ACTIVITIES, ASSIGNMENTS & ASSESSMENT

❑ Fluency Builders   1   2   3   4

❑ Reading Assignment: *J & J Language Readers* Unit 18, Book 1: *A Match for Chick*; Book 2: *The Hatch Back*; Book 3: *Fantastic Bash at Sunset*

❑ Independent Reading: _____
_____
_____

Mastery Tasks   1   2   3   4   5   6   7
            ❑   ❑   ❑   ❑   ❑   ❑   ❑

CONCEPTS & CONTENT	NOTES & EXAMPLES
❑ Six Traits of Effective Writing: Focus: • Ideas and Content • Organization • Voice • Word Choice • Sentence Fluency • Conventions ❑ Masterpiece Sentence Focus: Stages 1-5	_____ _____

WRITING & ENGLISH LANGUAGE ARTS

ACTIVITIES, ASSIGNMENTS & ASSESSMENT

❑ Composition Assignment: _____

_____

_____

Mastery Tasks   8   9   10   11   12

              ❑   ❑   ❑   ❑   ❑

Instructional Content

WORDS TO READ/SPELL

-atch	-itch	-utch	-etch	-otch
batch	ditch	clutch	etch	notch
catch	glitch	hutch	fetch	
hatch	hitch		sketch	
match	itch		stretch	
patch	itching			
watch	kitchen			
	pitch			
	stitch			
	switch			

EXPANDED WORD LIST

blotch	dispatch	last-ditch	pitching	snatch	splotch
botch	Dutch	mismatch	Scotch	snitch	stitching
crutch	hopscotch	pitcher	scratched	snitched	switch-hitting

FIVE FAVORITE IDIOMS OR EXPRESSIONS

1. _____

2. _____

3. _____

4. _____

5. _____

Tasks for Mastery

READING

Student Mastery Score	Minimum Mastery Score	Maximum Mastery Score
	16	20
80% or more correct, progress to next Task.		

TASK 1: **Phonemic Awareness**

Unit 18 words end with the /*ch*/ phoneme. They are spelled with final **-tch**. Write each of the vocabulary words from Unit 18. As you write the last three letters of each word, think about the single phoneme created by these three letters at the end of each **one-syllable word.**

1._____ 2._____ 3._____ 4._____ 5._____

6._____ 7._____ 8._____ 9._____ 10._____

11._____ 12._____ 13._____ 14._____ 15._____

16._____ 17._____ 18._____ 19._____ 20._____

Student Mastery Score	Minimum Mastery Score	Maximum Mastery Score
	29	36
80% or more correct, progress to next Task.		

TASK 2: Listening for Word Parts

A. Listen to each word. Print the word part your teacher repeats to you.

1. _____   2. _____   3. _____

4. _____   5. _____   6. _____

7. _____   8. _____   9. _____

10. _____   11. _____   12. _____

13. _____   14. _____   15. _____

16. _____   17. _____   18. _____

19. _____   20. _____   21. _____

22. _____   23. _____   24. _____

25. _____

B. Listen to each word. You will write part of each word. Your teacher will tell you which word parts to omit.

26. _____

27. _____

28. _____

29. _____

30. _____

31. _____

32. _____

33. _____

34. _____

35. _____

36. _____

Student Mastery Score	Minimum Mastery Score	Maximum Mastery Score
	23	29
80% or more correct, progress to next Task.		

TASK 3: **Nonphonetic Words**

The nonphonetic words in Level 1 (Units 1-18) are listed here. Look at each word. Say the word aloud. Then cover the word, and write it from memory in the blank below each word. When you finish, check your spelling.

two	were	they	should	you
_____	_____	_____	_____	_____
to	I	Ms.	do	into
_____	_____	_____	_____	_____
your	would	was	the	video
_____	_____	_____	_____	_____
many	Mr.	are	could	said
_____	_____	_____	_____	_____
of	taxi	any	Mrs.	put
_____	_____	_____	_____	_____
what	have	a	too	
_____	_____	_____	_____	

Student Mastery Score	Minimum Mastery Score	Maximum Mastery Score
	4	5
80% or more correct, progress to next Task.		

TASK 4: **Identifying Signal Words**

Read each question below. Decide whether the question is a Knowledge, Comprehension, Application, or Analysis question. Put an **X** in the box marked **K** if it is a Knowledge question. Put an **X** in the box marked **C** if it is a Comprehension question. Put an **X** in the box marked **Ap** if the question is an Application question. Put an **X** in the box marked **An** if it is an Analysis question. Underline the signal words.

K	C	Ap	An	
				1. Make a list of all the costumes mentioned in the story.
				2. Sort the costumes into different groups.
				3. What holiday was Miss Pitt telling the kids about at the beginning of the story?
				4. Tell about a parade you've seen.
				5. Predict who will have the funniest costume.

Student Mastery Score	Minimum Mastery Score	Maximum Mastery Score
	14	18
80% or more correct, progress to next Task.		

TASK 5: **Signal Word Sort**

Sort these signal words into the categories where they fit.

who   locate   summarize   use   tell   show

name   arrange   compare   paraphrase   classify   locate

choose   infer   generalize   identify   sort   explain

Knowledge	**Comprehension**	**Application**	**Analysis**
_____	_____	_____	_____
_____	_____	_____	_____
_____	_____	_____	_____
_____	_____	_____	_____
_____	_____		

SPELLING

Student Mastery Score	Minimum Mastery Score	Maximum Mastery Score
	17	21
80% or more correct, progress to next Task.		

TASK 6: **Spelling Word List**

Write the words that your teacher dictates on the Spelling Practice forms in the back of this book.

Student Mastery Score	Minimum Mastery Score	Maximum Mastery Score
	4	5
80% or more correct, progress to next Task.		

TASK 7: **Spelling Mastery Sentences**

Create five sentences containing some /*ch*/ words and nonphonetic words for everyone in the class to learn.

1. _____

2. _____

3. _____

4. _____

5. _____

ENGLISH/LANGUAGE ARTS

TASK 8: **Reviewing Main Verbs and Helping Verbs**

Student Mastery Score	Minimum Mastery Score	Maximum Mastery Score
	8	10
80% or more correct, progress to next Task.		

In the following sentences, an action verb is the main verb. Helping verbs are used with the action verb. They do not describe action. The following verbs can be used with action verbs to create a verb phrase:

am, are, is, was, were (forms of be)

has, had, have (forms of have)

do, did, does (forms of do)

Underline the verb phrase in the following sentences.

Examples:

I <u>did go</u> with you.

We <u>were singing</u>.

Max <u>is fixing</u> the dent.

You <u>have met</u> Bill.

1. I do drink the pop that mom gets at the store.

2. You are letting them win too many times.

3. Max Lutcher did plan the trip for anybody that wanted to go.

4. Sal was honking at him to get into the van.

5. Kit and Patrick were snacking on the hot pizza.

6. Miss Rich had sketched the map for the class.

7. Max and Mel have dragged the tent into the yard.

8. Kit, Tom, and Sal did wish that math would end.

9. Chick was fetching the black dog for us.

10. Dad does fix lunch for the kids at the kitchen table.

Student Mastery Score	Minimum Mastery Score	Maximum Mastery Score
	14	18
80% or more correct, progress to next Task.		

TASK 9: **Review—Nouns, Adjectives, and Verbs**

Use the following list of words to write 18 sentences. After you finish writing your sentences, draw:

A square around each noun

A circle around each verb

A triangle around each adjective

catch	match	batch	patch	latch	hatch
switch	stitch	itching	pitch	fetch	sketch
stretch	watch	clutch	notch	hutch	ditch

Example:

Max sits on the big black bench.

1. _____

2. _____

3. _____

4. _____

5. _____

6. _____

7. _____

8. _____

9. _____

10. _____

11. _____

12. _____

13. _____

14. _____

15. _____

16. _____

17. _____

18. _____

TASK 10: **Identifying Nouns, Adjectives, and Verbs**

Student Mastery Score	Minimum Mastery Score	Maximum Mastery Score
	12	15
80% or more correct, progress to next Task.		

Clip an article from a newspaper or magazine. Tape or paste it in the space provided on the page. In this article, identify at least five nouns, five verbs, and five adjectives. Be careful about the way the words are used. After you have identified the words in the sentences of your article, draw:

A square around each noun

A circle around each verb

A triangle around each adjective

Student Mastery Score	Minimum Mastery Score	Maximum Mastery Score
	8	10
80% or more correct, progress to next Task.		

TASK 11: **Idioms**

Words that do not mean exactly what they say are called idioms. Explain the meaning of each idiom.

1. dropoff _____

2. cut in _____

3. in a flash _____

4. split the difference _____

5. easy street _____

6. pumping iron _____

7. mask the problem _____

8. make a dent _____

9. eye-catching _____

10. catch-22 _____

Student Mastery Score	Minimum Mastery Score	Maximum Mastery Score
	8	10
80% or more correct, progress to next Task.		

TASK 12: **Morphology**

We will read each of the following sentences aloud. Think about the correct suffix for the word in each one. Then, write the correct word in the blank.

1. After Tim fell, they had to give him (crutch, crutches) _____ .

2. (Holland's, Hollands') _____ wetlands are fantastic.

3. Pat, the best athlete in our class, (catches, catch's) _____ with the left hand.

4. Pat also (pitches, pitch's) _____ with the right.

5. Al had (patched, patch) _____ his PC to Sam's.

6. In math, Mr. Nestor is the (stricter, strictest) _____ and the best.

7. They were (suspending, suspended) _____ from class.

8. After class, they (disinfect, disinfected) _____ the science kits.

9. I am (expecting, expected) _____ a quiz.

10. The kitchen sink was (stop, stopped) _____ up.

Spelling Practice

Name_____

Spell each reading and spelling vocabulary word correctly as your teacher reads it to you. Your teacher **will not score** the one word that you have crossed out.

1. _____   2. _____

3. _____   4. _____

5. _____   6. _____

7. _____   8. _____

9. _____   10. _____

11. _____   12. _____

13. _____   14. _____

15. _____   16. _____

17. _____   18. _____

19. _____   20. _____

21. _____   22. _____

23. _____   24. _____

25. _____   26. _____

27. _____   28. _____

29. _____   30. _____

Unit 13 spelling practice score: _____

Spelling Practice

Name_____

Spell each reading and spelling vocabulary word correctly as your teacher reads it to you. Your teacher **will not score** the one word that you have crossed out.

1. _____   2. _____

3. _____   4. _____

5. _____   6. _____

7. _____   8. _____

9. _____   10. _____

11. _____   12. _____

13. _____   14. _____

15. _____   16. _____

17. _____   18. _____

19. _____   20. _____

21. _____   22. _____

23. _____   24. _____

25. _____   26. _____

27. _____   28. _____

29. _____   30. _____

Unit 14 spelling practice score: _____

Spelling Practice

Name_____

Spell each reading and spelling vocabulary word correctly as your teacher reads it to you. Your teacher **will not score** the one word that you have crossed out.

1. _____ 2. _____

3. _____ 4. _____

5. _____ 6. _____

7. _____ 8. _____

9. _____ 10. _____

11. _____ 12. _____

13. _____ 14. _____

15. _____ 16. _____

17. _____ 18. _____

19. _____ 20. _____

21. _____ 22. _____

23. _____ 24. _____

25. _____ 26. _____

27. _____ 28. _____

29. _____ 30. _____

Unit 15 spelling practice score: _____

Spelling Practice

Name_____

Spell each reading and spelling vocabulary word correctly as your teacher reads it to you. Your teacher **will not score** the one word that you have crossed out.

1. _____   2. _____

3. _____   4. _____

5. _____   6. _____

7. _____   8. _____

9. _____   10. _____

11. _____   12. _____

13. _____   14. _____

15. _____   16. _____

17. _____   18. _____

19. _____   20. _____

21. _____   22. _____

23. _____   24. _____

25. _____   26. _____

27. _____   28. _____

29. _____   30. _____

Unit 16 spelling practice score: _____

Spelling Practice

Name_____

Spell each reading and spelling vocabulary word correctly as your teacher reads it to you. Your teacher **will not score** the one word that you have crossed out.

1. _____   2. _____

3. _____   4. _____

5. _____   6. _____

7. _____   8. _____

9. _____   10. _____

11. _____   12. _____

13. _____   14. _____

15. _____   16. _____

17. _____   18. _____

19. _____   20. _____

21. _____   22. _____

23. _____   24. _____

25. _____   26. _____

27. _____   28. _____

29. _____   30. _____

Unit 17 spelling practice score: _____

Spelling Practice

Name_____

Spell each reading and spelling vocabulary word correctly as your teacher reads it to you.
Your teacher **will not score** the one word that you have crossed out.

1. _____   2. _____

3. _____   4. _____

5. _____   6. _____

7. _____   8. _____

9. _____   10. _____

11. _____   12. _____

13. _____   14. _____

15. _____   16. _____

17. _____   18. _____

19. _____   20. _____

21. _____   22. _____

23. _____   24. _____

25. _____   26. _____

27. _____   28. _____

29. _____   30. _____

Unit 18 spelling practice score: _____